W9-CHH-237

Revised Edition
David Ortiz

By Jeff Savage

AMAZING
ATHLETES

Lerner Publications Company • Minneapolis

For Bailey Savage, my power-hitting son

Text copyright © 2010 by Jeff Savage

Lerner Publications Company
A division of Lerner Publishing Group, Inc.
241 First Avenue North
Minneapolis, MN 55401 U.S.A.

Website address: www.lernerbooks.com

Library of Congress Cataloging-in-Publication Data

Savage, Jeff, 1961–
    David Ortiz / by Jeff Savage. — Rev. ed.
       p.   cm. — (Amazing athletes)
    Includes bibliographical references and index.
    ISBN 978-0-7613-4920-4 (lib. bdg. : alk. paper)
    1. Ortiz, David, 1975– —Juvenile literature. 2. Baseball players—Dominican Republic—
Biography—Juvenile literature. I. Title.
GV865.O78S28 2010
796.357092—dc22 [B]   2008054981

Manufactured in the United States of America
1 2 3 4 5 6 – BP – 15 14 13 12 11 10

TABLE OF CONTENTS

The Red Sox play at Fenway Park in Boston.

SHINING STAR

David Ortiz and the Boston Red Sox were in trouble. They were playing in the 2008 American League Championship Series (ALCS) against the Tampa Bay Rays. Tampa Bay had already won three games in the series. If they won just one more game, Boston's season would be over. Tampa Bay would move on to the World Series. Even worse, the Rays had a seven-run lead after six innings. The Red Sox needed help from their biggest star.

The seventh inning started well for Boston. Shortstop Jed Lowrie drove a ball deep into right field for a double. The next two batters made outs, stranding Lowrie on second base. Centerfielder Coco Crisp was up next. He hit a single, moving Lowrie over to third base.

Coco Crisp gets a hit for the Red Sox.

Next was second baseman Dustin Pedroia's turn at bat. He swung hard and was rewarded with a single. Lowrie scored from third base for Boston's first run of the game, making the score 7–1. Boston was still way behind, but their big slugger was due up next.

David came to bat with Crisp on third base and Pedroia on first base. Red Sox fans screamed, "Papi! Papi!" Big Papi is David's nickname.

Rays pitcher Grant Balfour fired the ball toward home plate. David was ready. He took a mighty swing and made contact.

Grant Balfour pitches the ball late in the game.

David hits a home run in the seventh inning.

The crowd jumped to their feet as the ball sailed into the night sky. As Crisp and Pedroia ran toward home plate, the ball sailed over the wall in right field for a **home run**. The crowd roared and David's teammates celebrated in the **dugout**.

Boston still had a long way to go. David's home run made the score 7–4 with only two innings left in the game. But the Red Sox were up to the challenge. They scored three more runs in the eighth inning to tie the game. Then in the ninth, they capped their unlikely comeback with another run to win the game!

The Boston players were thrilled with their victory. "It was pretty much the most amazing thing I've ever been a part of," Crisp said, "to be down 7–0 in an elimination game and be able to come back." Big Papi and his teammates had done it!

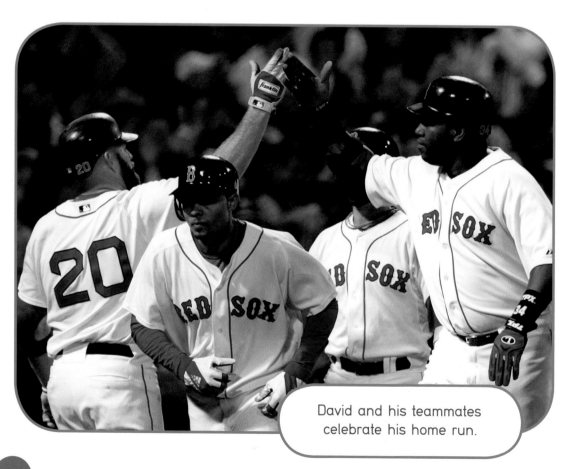

David and his teammates celebrate his home run.

Young boys play baseball in the Dominican Republic. Many Dominican kids grow up hoping to become Major League Baseball stars like David Ortiz.

GROWING UP HAPPY

David Américo Ortiz Arias was born November 18, 1975. His father's name is Américo. His mother's name is Angela Rosa Arias. David used the name Ortiz Arias until he was an adult.

David and his family grew up in the Dominican Republic. This country is part of a large island southeast of Florida in the Caribbean Sea. David's family lived in the country's capital, Santo Domingo.

David was a happy boy. He liked to laugh and joke around with his friends. He also liked to play sports. Baseball, basketball, and soccer were his favorites.

David grew up to be a big, strong kid. He was one of the best athletes in his neighborhood. David's best sport was baseball. He was a super hitter. He could smack the ball a long way.

Baseball is the most popular sport in the Dominican Republic. Children play the game on dirt fields. But many Dominican kids are too poor to buy bats and balls. So they use wooden sticks for bats and oranges for balls.

David was also a good basketball player. He was the best player on his team at Estudia Espallat High School. By this time, David was six feet four inches tall. He was so big and strong that most kids could not stop him from scoring baskets. David hoped he could become a pro athlete in one of his two favorite sports.

David is just one of many great baseball players from the Dominican Republic. David's former teammate Manny Ramirez is Dominican. Others include Vladimir Guerrero of the Los Angeles Angels, Albert Pujols of the St. Louis Cardinals, and Miguel Tejada of the Houston Astros.

David practices at first base while playing for the Wisconsin Timber Rattlers.

MAKING THE BIG LEAGUES

David wasn't quite good enough to become a pro basketball player. But he had all the skills to be a great baseball hitter. He had quick hands. They helped him swing the bat fast enough to hit fast pitches. And he was very strong. This helped him to hit the ball a long way.

Scouts for Major League Baseball teams watched David play in high school. They saw him hit long home runs. The Seattle Mariners liked David's skills. In 1992, the Mariners offered David a contract. He signed on to play for a Mariners team in the minor leagues. David had just turned 17 years old. He would have to work his way up to the major leagues.

Early in 1994, David moved to the United States. He joined a Mariner minor-league team in Arizona. He enjoyed two great seasons. In 1996, the Mariners sent David to play for their minor league team in Appleton, Wisconsin. Playing for the Wisconsin Timber Rattlers, he hit 34 doubles. He had a high batting average of .322 and smacked 18 home runs.

David and his wife, Tiffany, met when David was playing for the Timber Rattlers.

The Mariners traded David to the Minnesota Twins before the 1997 season. Around the same time, David dropped "Arias" from his name. He asked people to call him David Ortiz.

David had a huge year in 1997. He had a batting average over .300. In September, the Twins called him up to the major-league team. In his second game for the Twins, David smacked a double for his first major-league hit. A week later, he blasted his first home run. When the season ended, David had high hopes. He wanted to be the Twins' starting first baseman in 1998.

David (right) congratulates his teammate
Jacque Jones after Jones hit a home run.

HARD TIMES

The 1998 season started out great for David.
He began with a seven-game **hitting streak**.
But then, he broke his wrist. He couldn't play
for almost two months. But he played well
when he returned to the Twins.

David hoped to keep up his hot hitting in 1999. But he started out poorly in **spring training**. So the Twins sent him back to the minor leagues.

Playing for the Salt Lake Stingers, he cracked 30 home runs. He also led the league in **runs batted in (RBIs)**. But the Twins didn't call him up to the major leagues. He had to wait to get another chance.

David returned to the Twins in 2000. But playing for the Twins wasn't always fun. They were a losing team. They lost 93 games and won only 69.

David had some bad times with the Twins, but he kept smiling. He kept his good sense of humor. He was always telling jokes and making his teammates laugh. David was a very popular player. His teammates liked him, and Twins fans liked him.

David (left) walks back to the dugout with his teammate Bobby Kielty after Kielty hit a home run.

But things kept going wrong in Minnesota. In 2001, David broke his wrist again. He missed a lot of games. When he got back, he struggled. David finished the year with a low .234 batting average.

But the biggest disaster hit David after

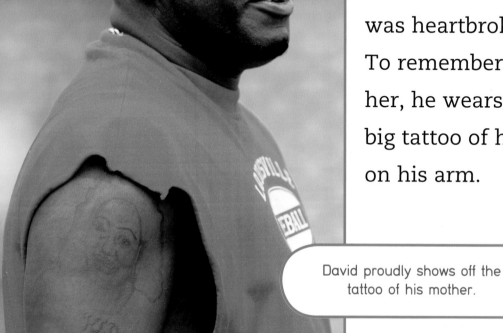

the season. His mother was killed in a car accident. David was heartbroken. To remember her, he wears a big tattoo of her on his arm.

David proudly shows off the tattoo of his mother.

The Twins turned things around in 2002. David hit 20 home runs, and the Twins won 94 games. The team made it to the **playoffs** for the first time in years. Minnesota beat the Oakland A's in an exciting American League **Division Series**. Then they lost to the Los Angeles Angels in the ALCS. It had been a fun year. But David wasn't sure he would be back with the Twins in 2003.

After losing a playoff game, David sits quietly in the dugout. The 2002 playoffs would be the last games David played for the Twins.

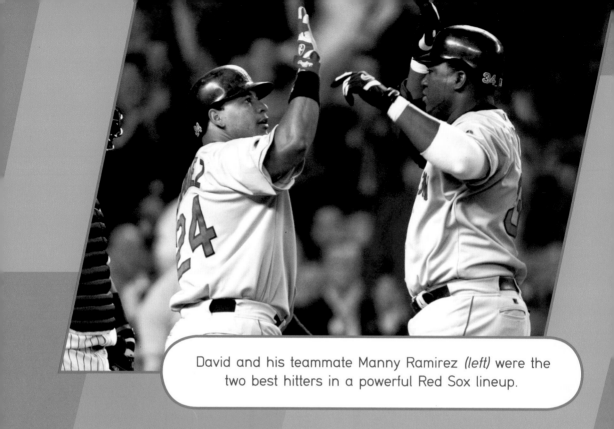

David and his teammate Manny Ramirez *(left)* were the two best hitters in a powerful Red Sox lineup.

WORLD SERIES WINNER

The Twins needed to save money on player salaries. So they let David become a **free agent**. Any team could take him. The Boston Red Sox signed him to a one-year contract for more than $1 million. David was thrilled to get a fresh start.

The Red Sox won 95 games in 2003 and made the playoffs. They faced the New York Yankees in the ALCS. The two teams battled for seven exciting games. But in the end, the Yankees won the series.

Red Sox players and fans were crushed. They had come so close to getting to the World Series! But David promised to keep trying. "I love Boston," David said. "I want to bring the fans a World Series title."

David became an instant fan favorite with the Red Sox. He is always happy to sign autographs for baseball fans.

David and his wife, Tiffany, have a home near Green Bay, Wisconsin. They live there with their daughters, Jessica and Alexandra, and son, D'Angelo.

The Red Sox knew they had a star in David Ortiz. Before the 2004 season, they signed him to a two-year contract for more than $12 million. David responded with a monster season in 2004. He batted .301 and hit 41 home runs. He also socked 47 doubles and added 139 runs batted in. The Red Sox won 98 games and a spot in the playoffs.

David hit a game-winning home run to beat the Los Angeles Angels in the Division Series. But the Yankees pounded on the Red Sox in the first three games of the ALCS. All seemed lost. No team had ever won a seven-game series after losing the first three games. But then David led them to wins in Games 4 and 5.

Suddenly, the Red Sox were on a roll. They needed two more wins to reach the World Series. Boston won with strong pitching in Game 6. Could they win Game 7?

In the first inning, David came to the plate with a runner on base. Bam! He crushed the ball for a home run! The Red Sox cruised to a 10–3 win. The Red Sox were going to the World Series!

David celebrates with his teammates after beating the Yankees in Game 7 of the ALCS.

David and his team faced the mighty St. Louis Cardinals. St. Louis had a bunch of super players, including first baseman Albert Pujols, center fielder Jim Edmonds, and third baseman Scott Rolen. But they were no match for Big Papi and the Red Sox.

The Red Sox beat up on the Cardinals and swept the series in four games. Boston had won the World Series! David and his teammates celebrated. The city of Boston exploded with joy. More than

David bashed a home run in his first at-bat in the 2004 World Series.

David celebrates with fans during a huge parade after the Red Sox World Series win.

one million fans came out to watch the Red Sox victory parade a few days later. David loved every minute of it.

David finished the 2005 season with his best year yet. He bashed 47 home runs and led the league with 148 runs batted in. The Red Sox made the playoffs but lost in the Division Series to the Chicago White Sox.

David celebrates a home run in 2007.

David did even better in 2006. He was first in the league with 54 home runs and 137 runs batted in. No hitter in baseball was more feared than Big Papi. David had a great year, but Boston failed to make the playoffs.

David finished the 2007 season with the fifth-best batting average and the fourth-most home runs in the American League. Big Papi was happy with his season. But the team's success was even more important. After knocking off the Los Angeles Angels and the Cleveland Indians, Boston faced the Colorado Rockies in the World Series. Once again the Red Sox proved to be the better team in the biggest series of the year. Boston swept the Rockies for their second World Series victory in four years.

The Red Sox celebrate their World Series victory against the Rockies.

David fought injuries throughout the 2008 season and didn't play as well as usual. The team still made the playoffs and beat the Angels in the Division Series. After their huge comeback win against the Rays in Game 5 of the ALCS, Boston went on to win Game 6 as well. But the team's luck ran out, and Tampa Bay won Game 7 to advance to the World Series.

After many struggles, David is having the time of his life. "I always believed in myself," he said. "What happened to me should teach everybody that you should never give up on anybody."

Young baseball fans really like David. They enjoy his smiling face and happy personality.

Selected Career Highlights

2008 Finished 18th in the American
League with 23 home runs

2007 Finished fourth in the American
League with 35 home runs

2006 Led the American League with 54 home runs
Led the American League with 137
runs batted in
Finished third in voting for American League
Most Valuable Player

2005 Won Hank Aaron Award for best
all-around hitter in the American League
Led the American League with 148 runs
batted in
Finished second in the American League with 47 home runs
Finished second in voting for American League Most Valuable
Player

2004 In 14 playoff games, batted .400 with 5 home runs, 19 runs batted
in, and 13 runs scored
Finished fourth in the American League Most Valuable Player
(MVP) voting
Named the American League Championship Series MVP
Named the Red Sox Most Valuable Player
Won the Edgar Martinez Award as the league's best designated hitter
Finished second in the American League with 47 doubles
Finished second in the American League with 41 home runs
Finished second in the American League with 139 runs batted in

2003 Finished fifth in the American League MVP voting
Hit a major-league-career-high 31 home runs
Earned a major-league-career-high 101 runs batted in

2002 Had a career-best 19-game hitting streak

2001 Had first career two-home run game against the Texas Rangers

2000 Hit first career grand slam against the Boston Red Sox

1999 Playing for the Salt Lake Stingers, led the Pacific Coast League in
runs batted in with 110

1997 Named the Minnesota Twins Minor League Player of the Year

Glossary

American League Championship Series (ALCS): a series of games played to decide the winner of the American League. The team that wins four games in the series goes on to the World Series.

batting average: a number that describes how often a baseball player makes a base hit

contract: a written agreement between a player and team

Division Series: the first round of the Major League Baseball playoffs

double: a two-base hit

dugout: the area next to the field where a baseball team sits

free agent: a player who is free to sign with any team

hitting streak: hitting safely in a number of games in a row

home run: a hit that lets the batter circle the bases, cross home plate, and score a run. Home runs are sometimes called homers.

Major League Baseball: the top two professional baseball leagues in North America, the National League and the American League

minor leagues: groups of teams in which players improve their skills and prepare to move to the majors

playoffs: games played to decide which team is the Major League Baseball champion

runs batted in (RBIs): the number of runners able to score on a batter's action, such as a hit or a walk

scouts: in baseball, people who judge the skills of players

single: a one-base hit

spring training: a time from February through March when baseball teams train for the season

World Series: baseball's championship. The winning teams from the National League and American League meet each other in the World Series.

Further Reading & Websites

Savage, Jeff. *Albert Pujols*. Minneapolis: Lerner Publications Company, 2007.

Stewart, Mark. *The Boston Red Sox*. Chicago: Norwood House Paper Editions, 2008.

Stewart, Mark. *Long Ball: The Legend and Lore of the Home Run*. Minneapolis: Millbrook Press, 2006.

Boston Red Sox: The Official Site
http://boston.redsox.mlb.com
The official website of the Boston Red Sox includes the team schedule and results, late-breaking news, biographies of past and present players and coaches, and much more.

Major League Baseball: The Official Site
http://mlb.mlb.com
Major League Baseball's official website provides fans with the latest scores and game schedules, as well as information on players, teams, and baseball history.

Sports Illustrated Kids
http://www.sikids.com
The *Sports Illustrated Kids* website covers all sports, including baseball.

Index

Photo Acknowledgments

The photographs in this book are reproduced courtesy of: © Christian Petersen/Getty Images, p. 4; © Jim Rogash/Getty Images, p. 5, 8; © Elsa/Getty Images, p. 6, 26; © Jim McIsaac/Getty Images, p. 7; AP Photo/Wide World Photos, p. 9, 15, 17, 19, 21, 23, 28; Wisconsin Timber Rattlers, p. 12; © Darren McCollester/Stringer/Getty Images, p. 14; Minnesota Twins, p. 16; © Chuck Rydlewski/Icon SMI, p. 18; © Mike Segar/Reuters/CORBIS, p. 20; © Shawn Best/Reuters/CORBIS, p. 24; © Jessica Rinaldi/Reuters/CORBIS, p. 25; © Stephen Dunn/Getty Images, p. 27; Jack Maley/Boston Red Sox, p. 29.

Front Cover: © J. Meric/Getty Images